STYLISH *Découpage*

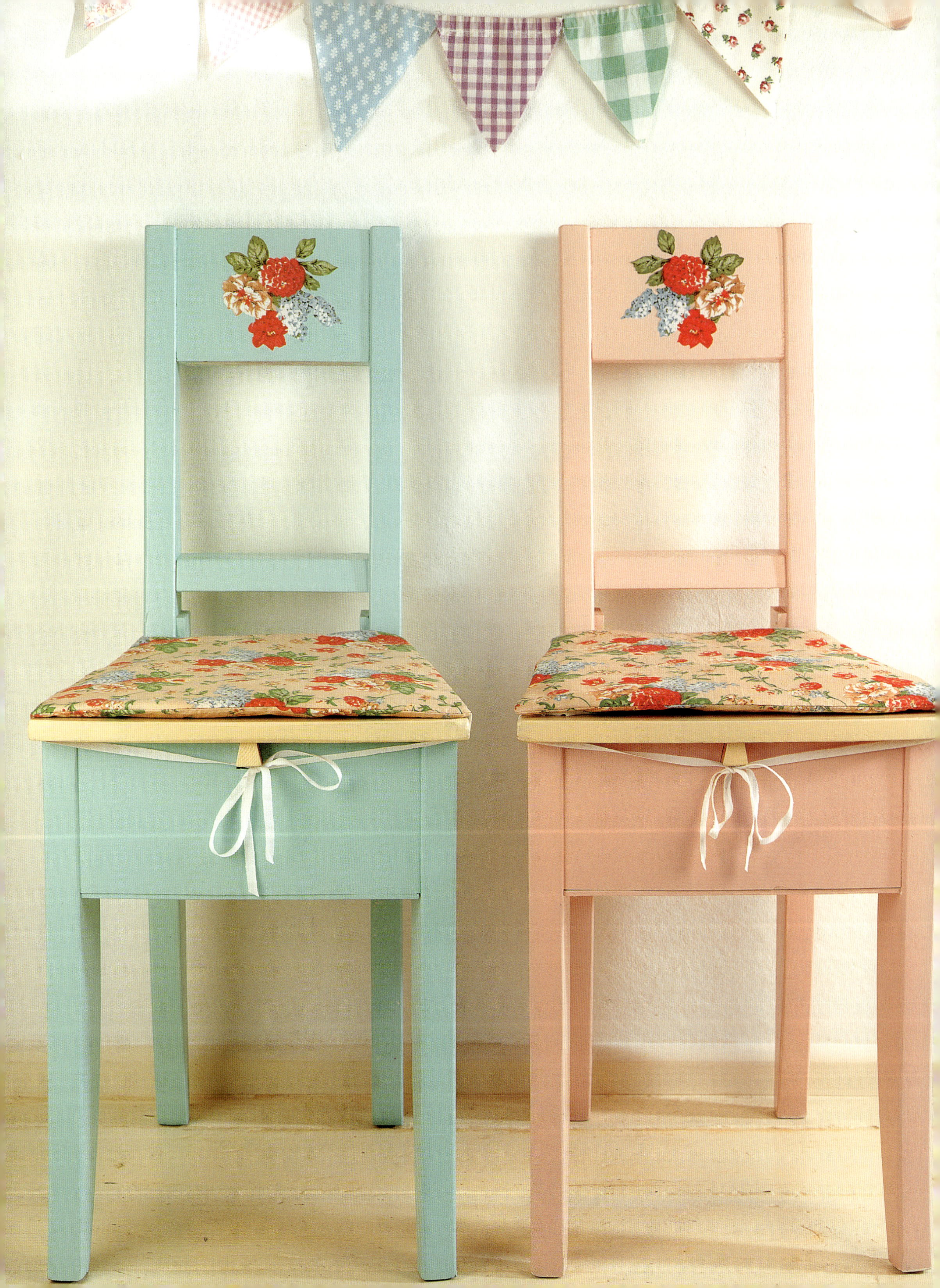

STYLISH

Découpage

15 step-by-step projects to dazzle and delight

MARY MAGUIRE

NEW HOLLAND

First published in 2004 by New Holland Publishers (UK) Ltd
London • Cape Town • Sydney • Auckland

Garfield House, 86–88 Edgware Road, London W2 2EA, United Kingdom
www.newhollandpublishers.com

80 McKenzie Street, Cape Town 8001, South Africa

14 Aquatic Drive, Frenchs Forest, NSW 2086, Australia

218 Lake Road, Northcote, Auckland, New Zealand

ISBN 1 84330 828 2

3 5 7 9 10 8 6 4 2

Senior Editor: Clare Hubbard
Editor: Anna Southgate
Production: Hazel Kirkman
Design: AG&G Books; Glyn Bridgewater and Jane Skinner
Photography: Shona Wood
Editorial Direction: Rosemary Wilkinson

Reproduction by Pica Digital Pte Ltd, Singapore
Printed and bound in Malaysia by Times Offset (M) Sdn. Bhd.

CONTENTS

PROJECTS

INTRODUCTION

Découpage is one of the easiest crafts to master, and although it is basically cut and paste, it can be elevated to a fine art through practice, skill, and creativity, just like any other craft.

Traditionally, découpage was finished with up to twenty layers of varnish. Each layer would have been sanded before the next was applied, so that a smooth, glossy, lacquerlike finish was achieved. There would be no irregularities on the surface and the pasted-on print

Right: **This screen has been decorated with shapes cut from origami paper (see page 59).**

could be passed off as a painting. The practice originated in Italy, where it was called *lucca contraffatta* (imitation lacquer). The Italians discovered that hand coloring prints and pasting them onto furniture helped satisfy the demand for the considerably more expensive hand-painted works of great artists. They perfected the technique until it became an art form. Its popularity spread throughout Europe, and it became a common pastime for ladies, even nobility: Marie Antoinette is said to have been fond of cutting up her oil paintings and pasting them onto furniture. In fact, the word "découpage" is French.

Above: **In addition to the MDF blanks available at craft stores, there is a wide range of objects that make ideal surfaces for découpage. Small sets of wooden drawers are inexpensive, nicely proportioned and very useful. Shoe boxes are easy to get ahold of and make very nice gifts, once decorated. Scour thrift stores to find unusual items such as lampshades and crockery.**

The craft reached the height of its popularity during the Victorian era, when cheap, mass-produced printed images became available to a wider market. It was so popular that partially cutout images were manufactured specifically for découpage. Many of the designs are still being produced today and some of them appear in this book.

This book offers a series of projects for both novice and advanced découpage artists. Many of them use medium density fiberboard (MDF) blanks, which are made for decorating and are available in craft and hobby stores. The same techniques can also be applied to old or secondhand items, provided that all the necessary preparation is carried out beforehand. The advantage of MDF is that it has a smooth finish, no grain, and is stable. For the most part, the projects in this book move away from the old, antiqued look often associated with découpage in favor of a brighter, breezier approach, using a wide range of fresh pastel-colored paints and floral imagery. Today, most of us are happy to use découpage purely decoratively. We don't want to pretend it is painted on, so the laborious process of applying twenty coats of varnish is not necessary, as long as you make sure you apply enough coats to protect your prints from wear and tear.

Choosing, cutting, and creating designs is a fun and relaxing way to spend your time. All sorts of objects can be used as a base, either as an embellishment for your own home or as a gift for someone. Interesting images can be found in magazines and old books, on seed packets, paper napkins, letters, maps, and wrapping paper. You can use copyright-free source books, CDs, or Victorian scraps. There is plenty to choose from. Do respect the copyright laws, however, which are there to protect originators from having their images exploited. Most publishers will be happy to give you permission provided you are not manufacturing items for sale.

MATERIALS

You can use wallpaper, old book illustrations, letters, musical manuscripts, postcards—the list goes on. If you are reluctant to use originals, scan or color copy them.

1. Wallpaper: Look through wallpaper books to find interesting and funky designs. Ask your local supplier to keep old sample books for you.

2. Wrapping paper: This is probably the most accessible and widely used source material for découpage. It is the right thickness and is available in an abundance of designs.

3. Paper napkins: These have recently become very popular for découpage, and the range of designs is now far greater than ever before. They often have a festive theme, so collect them when you see them as stocks will change to suit the season.

4. Découpage papers: Some craft stores stock papers specially designed for découpage. Designs include musical manuscripts, antique handwriting, and images of fishes and birds.

5. Color copies and printouts: If you don't want to use an original image, you can take it to your local copy store, where they will color copy it for you (although this can be expensive). Alternatively, if you have a good scanner and printer, you can do it yourself. Experiment with different kinds of paper to find out which are the best to use. Fabric, feathers, and leaves can also be scanned or copied, but be careful not to scratch the surface of the scanner or copier.

6. Stickers: These can also be used in découpage, as long as they can be varnished over. Test them first.

7. Victorian scraps: There is a wide variety still being produced today (see pages 78–79 for suppliers). These charming embossed images are already partially cut out, which makes them very easy to use .

8. Foils: Keep your candy wrappers! Smoothed out, they will make a great source material for your designs.

9. Copyright-free source books and CDs: Books and CDs containing copyright-free images are available on all sorts of subjects, including Christmas, animals etc. (see pages 78–79 for details).

10. Origami papers: These small, square sheets of paper tend to have miniature patterns, making them ideal for découpage; see the variation of the Sky Screen on page 59.

STORAGE

It is useful to be able to store any unused cutout for a later date. Plastic-covered pages from a photo album are ideal for this purpose. They will hold the shapes flat and protect them from dust and damage.

1
2
3
4
5
6
7
8
9
10

EQUIPMENT

You don't need a lot of equipment for découpage, but if you are intending to do a lot of it, invest in good-quality brushes, scissors, a cutting mat, and a craft knife.

Note: When using any equipment, you should always follow the manufacturer's instructions.

1. Muslin: This fine, open-weave, cotton cloth is ideal for wiping newly sanded surfaces.

2. Brushes: Iinvest in good-quality brushes if you intend to make a hobby of this craft; they won't shed hairs.

3. Roller/brayer: This is useful for flattening down your pasted design and getting rid of any trapped air bubbles.

4. Sponge: You will need a clean, soft sponge for wiping over a freshly pasted design to remove any surplus paste.

5. Fine brushes: Good-quality, fine-headed brushes with broad, flat, blunt ends are especially useful.

6. Plastic wrap: This is handy for covering surfaces in order to protect them from paint, but also for covering pots of paint and paste mixtures to prevent them from drying out as you work.

7. Face mask: Wear one of these for protection against sanding dust, stray powder particles, and fumes when you spray varnish.

8. Sponge spreaders: These are useful for spreading paste. Beneath the sponge head, there is a firm plastic core that gives the tool more body.

9. Knife: It is good to have a slim, blunt-ended knife for peeling off unsatisfactory prints.

10. Plastic wallets: These are very useful for storing images.

11. Protractor, pencil, and ruler: You will need these for planning out your designs. Choose a hard pencil and make sure the point is sharp.

12. Reusable putty: This is invaluable for positioning images. It enables you to tack elements of your design into place so that you can look at them from a distance.

13. Craft Knife: A craft knife is important for cutting out tiny interior areas that are difficult to reach using scissors. Make sure you always use a sharp blade, as blunt ones tend to tear or buckle the paper.

14. Cutting mat: If you do craft work often, you will find a cutting mat useful. Otherwise, improvise with a piece of cardboard, linoleum, or a thick wad of newspaper.

15. Scissors: You will need a pair of scissors with fine, sharp points. Embroidery scissors are good for cutting out fine detail. You will also need a large pair of paper or general-purpose scissors for cutting out larger areas. Keep both of these specially dedicated to découpage.

16. Spatula: Use to smooth out freshly pasted prints and to get rid of any trapped air bubbles.

17. Decorators' and masking tape: Decorators' tape is a smooth-surfaced low-tack tape, while masking tape has a slightly crinkled surface. They are both used to mask out areas for painting and for achieving straight lines.

18. Lining paper: Be sure to have a large supply of lining paper, scrap, or newspaper before you start a project. A new sheet for each pasting is the best way to avoid mishaps.

19. Lazy Susan: A lazy Susan is a round wooden board that revolves on a smaller base. It is very useful for doing craft work, as you can turn your artwork without needing to touch it. A lazy Susan is particularly useful for varnishing—just be sure to cover it with plastic wrap or foil before you start.

20. Mixing bowl: Use old bowls for mixing paint and paste. Plastic ones are good and easy to clean.

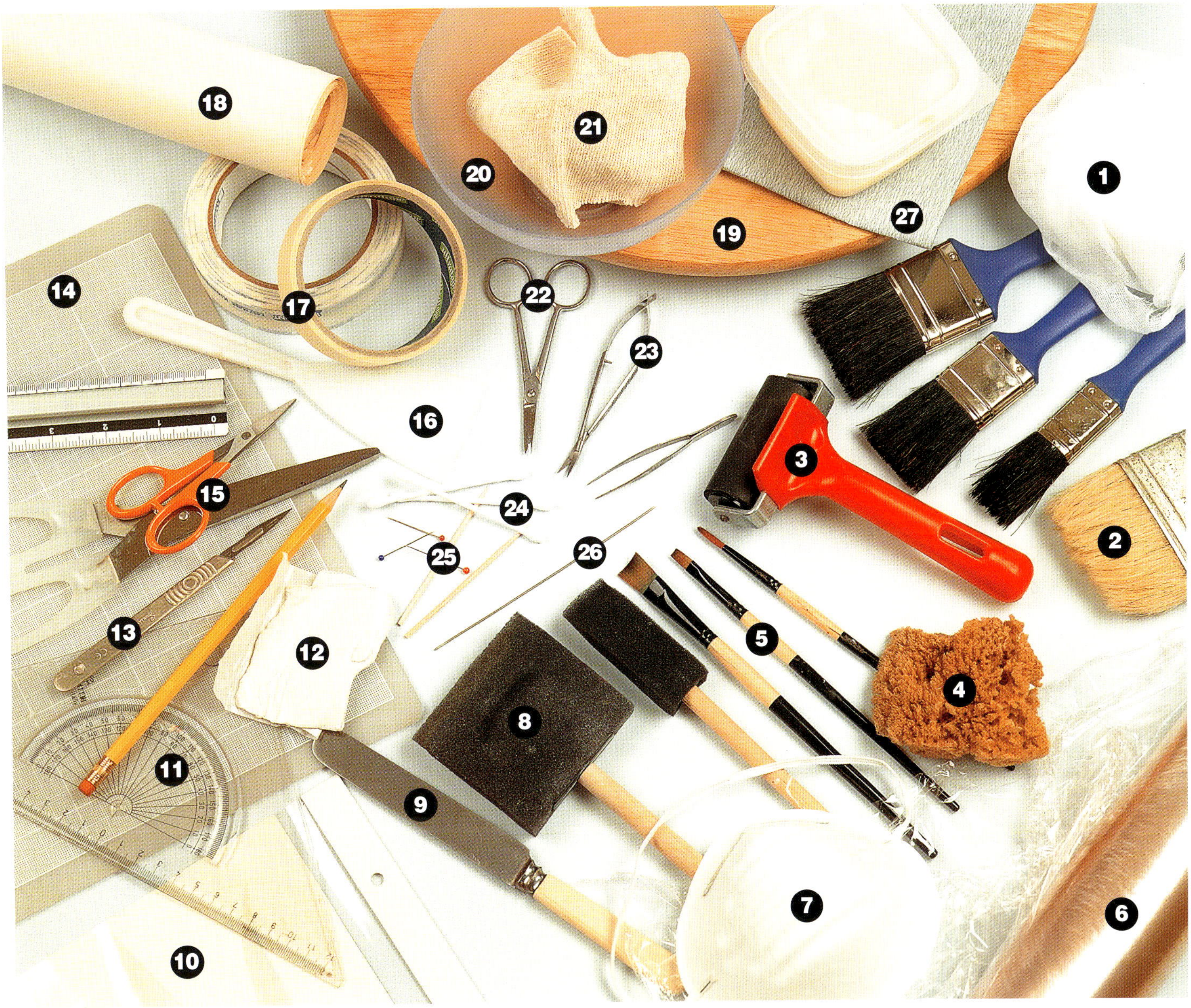

21. Cloths: Keep a pile of old cotton cloths around as you are working so that you can mop up spills and wipe paintbrushes with minimum effort.

22. Manicure scissors: These are good for cutting out fine detail. They often have curved edges, which can be ideal. Keep them solely for this purpose!

23. Tweezer scissors: The squeezing action of these very sharp, tweezerlike scissors, ensures a fine, smooth cut. They are available with both straight and curved points (see pages 78–79 for suppliers).

24. Cotton swabs: These are very useful for dabbing away little pockets of glue that collect in awkward places.

25. Cocktail sticks and pins: These can be useful for applying tiny amounts of glue.

26. Dollmaker's needle: This needle is long and straight enough to go through an egg, while the eye is big enough to thread thin ribbon through.

27. Sandpaper: Available at hardware and home improvement stores, it comes in a range of gauges from coarse to very fine. For sanding between layers of paint, use a very fine paper; for stripping off old paint, use a coarse paper.

PAINTS, PASTES, AND VARNISHES

Many different kinds of paint can be used for découpage. I've chosen to use emulsions as they come in a wide range of colors and can be bought inexpensively in small tester sizes.

Note: When using any product, you should always follow the manufacturer's instructions.

1. Spray varnish: Although this is more expensive than conventional varnish, it is quicker to apply and the drying time is very fast. It is available in matte, gloss, and satin finishes. The projects in this book were made using either Plaka matte varnish or a triple gloss varnish.

2. Decorators' varnish: This product has been devised specially for fine decorative finishes. It is a thin, milky, water-based liquid, available in a flat, satin, and gloss finishes.

3. Tissue paste: This is a light paste, manufactured solely for use with napkins.

4. High-gloss varnish: Most of the projects were created using water-based paints and varnishes. For a really glossy finish a varnish devised for polymer clay is recommended.

5. Wallpaper paste: Although useful for projects made with wallpaper, this is also good for making up your own découpage paste mix (see page 19 for details).

6. White school glue: This general-purpose glue can be used alone on heavier papers or mixed with wallpaper paste for use on lighter papers.

7. Sticks: These are extremely useful for mixing paints and paste. Make sure they are smooth and will not shed bits of bark into your paint.

8. Bronze powders: These are extremely fine metallic powders, which can be mixed with a special medium, glue, or varnish to give a metallic finish or luster to a piece. They are available in a large range of colors including purple, green, and blue.

9. Three-dimensional paints: These squeezable bottles of paint come complete with nozzle lids that enable you to pipe out decoration. The paint stays raised once dry—like icing—and gives an embossed effect to your work. They are available in a range of colors and finishes, including metallic, pearl, and sparkle. They are available from craft stores.

10. Acrylic paint: These small pots of paint can be used to paint eggs. They come in a range of pretty, pale pastel colors.

11. Primers: Use white primer for projects with light finishes and gray for darker ones. I have used water-based primers, which are suitable to go under emulsion paints and are easier to wash out of brushes.

12. Felt-tip pens: If you want to add a bit more color to your prints, to color in black and white prints, or to make the white edges of cutouts disappear, you can use felt-tip pens. You can get these in subtle colors from good art-supply stores. Before using them, test them out with paste and varnish to make sure the colors don't bleed.

13. Emulsion paints: Available in a much wider selection of colors than oil-based paints, these have the added advantage of being available in small tester pots. These water-based paints are relatively quick-drying. They are easy to use but must be protected using a varnish.

PREPARING THE IMAGES

Before you start, it is essential that you have a good pair of sharp scissors. Furthermore, any paper that isn't colorfast will need to be sprayed first with a fixative or varnish.

This will ensure that the colors don't bleed during the gluing or varnishing stages. Hold the can 8 in. away from the paper and spray evenly over the surface. A great trick is to spray very lightweight papers, which makes them more robust for cutting and pasting.

ISOLATING IMAGERY

When cutting an image from a busy pattern, it helps to isolate it first by drawing around it.

CUTTING OUT INTERIOR AREAS

Small, detailed areas are best cut out before the whole isolated image is cut from a sheet of paper. This will give you greater stability and reduces the risk of tearing. Use a self-healing mat and a craft knife. Check that the blade is sharp—a blunt blade will tear the paper. (See photo above right.)

GENERAL CUTTING

Cut out an isolated image using a medium-to-large pair of scissors. Take care not to cut across any image you might want to use later (see photo right).

CUTTING EDGES

You will need to use a small pair of scissors for cutting the final outlined edges of an isolated image. Manicure scissors are good for this. Practice on magazine images. Cut around your shape, directing the scissors from beneath the paper so that only the points are visible. This will make it easier for you to see where you are cutting. Hold the scissors with a relaxed hand, tilted upward (gives the edge of the paper a slight bevel). Guide the paper into the blades, reserving the tips for intricate edges. Every so often, cut off surplus paper and discard. (See photo right.)

CUTTING CURVES TO FIT OBJECTS

There are two ways of doing this. The first is by placing your object on top of the print in the desired position, and tracing along the curve with a pencil. This can then be cut. The second method, shown here, is to tack the image into position, use your finger to rub along the edge of your object—its shape will be embossed onto the paper—and then you can cut it out.

INTERLOCKING IMAGES

If your final composition involves several different shapes that touch each other, you may want to make sure that the images line up neatly without gaps instead of merely overlapping. This can be done quite simply by cutting an excess amount at the end of each shape at the point at which it should meet another. Line two such shapes up on the cutting surface, each with a slight overlap. Stabilize them with tiny bits of reusable putty, and cut through both overlapping prints along the line you want to join.

Make sure your blade is sharp and that you cut through both prints completely. You will need to press down firmly to secure the prints and prevent any movement.

THICKENING FINE LINES

This is a useful tip for helping to cut out fine lines. Before cutting, choose a crayon or felt-tip pen (make sure it is colorfast) the same color as the image to be cut out and color around fine lines to thicken them up. (See photo below.)

LOSING WHITE EDGES

If your cutout images are dark and they are going to be stuck onto dark backgrounds, the white edges of the paper will show up. To get rid of these white edges, use a color felt-tip pen or crayon that matches either the print or the background. Check first for colorfast compatibility with your varnish.

COMPOSITION

Beauty is in the eye of the beholder and only you can decide what composition will please you. Spend time shuffling your prints around until you achieve an appealing arrangement.

Don't rush this process—it's better to spend time getting it right at this stage rather than having to peel off an unsatisfactory design later on.

BACKGROUND

For a design with many different elements, first decide what is going to be used as the background. This will tend to be the largest of your cutouts. Tack down this image first, using reusable putty.

CREATING A RHYTHM

Build up the design with smaller elements. Here, smaller blossoms have been added to give the design a circular or wreathlike quality.

FOREGROUND ELEMENTS

Start to place the elements in the foreground, tacking them in place with reusable putty as you go. Be careful not to overwhelm the background. Generally, more detailed images will be in the foreground. (See photo right.)

MARKING POSITIONS

Using a sharp pencil, lift the edges of the tacked prints slightly away from the surface so that you can mark their positions with a dotted line—just to the inside of where the edge will lie—so once pasted, the marks will not show.

PASTING AN IMAGE

Once you are certain of a composition and have it clearly marked out on your object, you can begin to paste the prints into position.

Always use a new sheet of newspaper for each pasting. The thickness of the glue you use will depend on what type of paper you are gluing—a heavier, thicker paper will require a thicker paste, while tissue paper needs a thinner mix. Many of the découpage glues on the market have a PVA base.

MIX A PASTE

Following the manufacturer's instructions, mix up some wallpaper paste in a jar or pot with a fitted lid (you will probably only need to use a fraction of the packet depending on how much découpage you are doing). Once this is mixed, add roughly an equal quantity of glue and mix thoroughly until the two are completely blended. The wallpaper paste will give the resulting mix a more slimy texture; this allows more leeway when positioning the prints, as white school glue tends to adhere too quickly.

APPLYING THE PASTE

Lay the print, image-side down, on a sheet of scrap paper and spread the glue evenly, making sure that it reaches all edges. Don't worry if you go over the edges, but don't move your print as the paste may get onto the front of the image and pull off the surface color. Set the print into position. Smooth it out from the center with your fingers. Use a spatula to help spread the image and to force out any excess glue. Be careful not to press too heavily, or you may scrape off the surface of your print. (See photo above.)

REMOVING EXCESS GLUE

Remove excess glue by wiping over your object with a barely damp sponge. Repeat until all the surface glue has been removed. (See photo above right.)

TRAPPED GLUE

Any paste trapped in "cutaway islands" can be removed with the tip of a cotton swab.

VARNISHING

For most of the projects in this book, four coats of varnish will be sufficient. However, some items will need more protection from wear and tear, so allow at least six coats.

The Polka Dot Tray (see page 48) and the Chintz Chairs (see page 64) are examples of items that will need at least six coats. If you want to achieve a finely lacquered finish, you will need to sand between the layers of varnish. To achieve a smooth surface, rub harder over any areas where there are lumps or dust, but take great care not to rub through to your design. Wipe off any dust particles with a soft, barely damp cloth. Once dry, repeat the process, sanding between every second coat until you have the surface you are happy with.

Spray varnishes speed up the process. They are more expensive, but are better for irregular shapes such as eggs. Whether you use a water-based or oil-based matte, satin, or gloss varnish is mostly a matter of taste. Experiment on leftover print scraps. Polyurethane tends to darken prints and yellows slightly with age, which can be good if you want an antique effect.

APPLYING VARNISH

It is important to remember that many thin coats of varnish are better than a few thick ones.

Apply your varnish with a good-quality, flat, blunt-ended brush that will not shed hairs. Choose the size in relation to the object you are working on. Dip the tip of the brush into the varnish; don't overload it, as it will drip. Hold the brush at a forty-degree angle. Lightly drag the brush over the surface of your object. Work away from the center of the piece in the same direction as the wood grain, leaving a smooth, even coat. Then allow to dry thoroughly. Find a box large enough to cover your object to protect it from dust while it is drying.

VARNISHING AN EGG

If you don't want to use a spray varnish (see right), place reusable putty over the holes in the egg and insert a pushpin in the hole at each end. Use these to support and revolve the egg on a reel of tape as shown. Check that the egg clears the surface.

USING A LAZY SUSAN

A lazy Susan can come in handy when varnishing. You can turn an object without getting fingerprints on it. Cover it with a piece of foil or cling film to protect its surface while you work.

SPRAY VARNISHING

When using a spray varnish, it is useful to put your object on the lazy Susan, and place it inside a cardboard box. (Suspend eggs from the top of the box.) Wear a face mask to protect yourself from fumes. Slowly revolve the stand as you spray. The box will help stop the varnish particles from dispersing and will prevent dust from settling on your object.

TROUBLESHOOTING

Take care with each stage of a project and try not to rush any of the processes involved. This way you will avoid making mistakes.

It is advisable to test the compatibility of your materials from the start. (Will the paper react to the glue? Does it stretch terribly? Does the varnish change its color or opacity?) Most mistakes are easily rectified, and if they can't be, then you can always add other smaller images over the top to camouflage them.

AIR BUBBLES

If an air bubble forms while you are gluing, gently peel back the print until you reach the bubble. Apply a little more glue, and using a spatula, ease the print back into place. If you discover the air bubble after the print is dry, use a sharp craft knife and cut along the nearest contour in your design to reach it. Lift the print carefully with the edge of your craft knife and apply some glue to the underside with a cocktail stick or pin. Then ease the print down, stroking out any air, and wiping away excess glue with a damp sponge. Allow it time to dry completely.

TEARS

Generally when a wet print tears, it doesn't happen in a straight line, but in a crooked line, usually with one side of the tear showing the white underside of the paper. This actually makes it easier to repair. Peel away the area involved and then repaste the torn side with the visible underside first. Apply minimal glue along this white edge, and place the other half of the tear on top, matching up the design. Lightly smooth it into place with a damp cloth, taking care not to move it out of alignment.

PEELING IMAGES

This tends to happen along the edges of an image where insufficient paste has been used. Take a craft knife and lift the peeling edge slightly, then force some glue underneath with a pin, brush, or cocktail stick. Press down firmly and maintain pressure for some time. Wipe away any excess glue. It may be necessary to place a weight (such as a telephone book) over the area to ensure the edge stays down. Always place a piece of cloth over the image first, however, to protect it.

REMOVING A PRINT

If before varnishing you decide you don't like your design, don't despair. You can completely remove it. Use a warm, damp sponge or cotton swab to soften the glue at the edges of an image first. Then, using a fine, blunt edge, such as a spatula or palette knife, slide under the image and gently lift it little by little. Continue working in this way until you have completely removed the design. Any paper residue can be sanded off once the object is dry again.

PATCHWORK FRAME

This project uses a napkin with a pretty pink patchwork design. If you cannot find something similar, you can create your own patches by cutting up squares of different patterned paper and fitting them together. Alternatively, you could use fabric, but be sure to use fine, tightly woven cotton.

YOU WILL NEED

- Paper napkin
- Wooden mirror frame
- Pencil and ruler
- Cutting surface and craft knife
- Water-based primer
- Paintbrushes
- Masking tape (optional)
- Hot pink and pastel pink emulsion paints
- Fine sandpaper
- Face mask
- Muslin cloth
- Paste (see page 19)
- Sponge spreader
- Cloth
- Roller
- Water-based varnish

1 Measure the napkin against your wooden frame and figure out what size border you will need to fit it. Then cut out the center of the napkin on your cutting surface, using a craft knife and ruler. Prime the wooden frame.

2 Once dry, use a pencil and ruler to mark where you want your inner and outer painted borders to be. For crisp lines, use masking tape to protect the areas you do not want painted. Color the inner border first, using the hot pink emulsion paint, making sure you don't forget the inner edge.

3 Paint the outer border, including the outside edge of the frame. When dry, give the paint a light sand, wipe away any dust with a muslin cloth, and apply a second coat to each border.

4 Remove the backing layers of tissue from the napkin. Apply paste to the appropriate area of the painted frame using a sponge spreader.

5 Carefully lay the print in position. Smooth out the tissue very gently with your fingers, being careful not to tear the paper. Lay a barely damp cloth over the print and roll across it with the roller. Cut a motif from the leftover napkin and place in each corner of the frame.

6 Once the tissue is dry, paint pastel pink stripes around both borders and leave to dry. Apply six coats of varnish, sanding between layers two and four.

LETTER RACK

Remind yourself of vacations on distant shores with this letter rack. Save postcards of your favorite places or collect vintage cards. You don't have to use the original; you can color copy or scan and print them, reducing them by 50 percent in size to fit your project.

YOU WILL NEED

- MDF blank letter rack
- Fine sandpaper
- Face mask
- Muslin cloth
- Water-based primer
- Paintbrushes
- Blue emulsion paint
- Selection of vacation postcards
- Scissors
- Reusable putty
- Pencil and ruler
- Paste (see page 19)
- Sponge
- Water-based varnish

1 Lightly sand the blank letter rack and wipe off any dust with a muslin cloth. Prime the piece and leave to dry, then paint with two layers of blue emulsion. Sand between dry coats to get a really smooth finish.

2 Scan your postcards and reduce them 50 percent in size. Print out or color copy the images and cut them out using a pair of scissors.

3 Using reusable putty, tack your prints to the letter rack at jaunty angles until you have achieved a pleasing arrangement. Mark out the positions using a sharp pencil and ruler.

4 Paste each postcard into place, carefully using a damp sponge to smooth out the images and remove excess glue. Allow to dry. Once the glue is dry, apply four layers of varnish, sanding after each second coat.

ARTIST'S TIP

Fifties postcards can be bought cheaply from swap meets and thrift stores.

DESIGN VARIATION

For a totally different effect, paint the letter rack in a pale color and use images of angels.

SCRUMPTIOUS PLATTER

Bronze powders give a metallic luster to this MDF blank plate. Chocolates shapes, cut from a sheet of wrapping paper, have been used for decoration, but you could also use images from advertisements in magazines. The surface on the plate has been finished with a spray gloss varnish. Take care when you clean this piece—use a damp cloth and don't put it in the dishwasher!

YOU WILL NEED

- MDF blank plate
- Fine sandpaper
- Face mask
- Muslin cloth
- Water-based primer
- Paintbrushes
- Russet emulsion paint
- White school glue
- Bronze powders (fire copper and purple)
- Chocolate wrapping paper
- Scissors
- Colored pencil or felt-tip pen
- Pencil
- Paste (see page 19)
- Sponge
- Spray gloss varnish

1 Lightly sand the MDF blank until smooth all over and wipe off any dust with a muslin cloth. Prime the plate and leave it to dry.

2 Apply two coats of emulsion, sanding between the dry layers.

3 Mix a thin solution of glue and fire copper bronze powder and lightly brush it around the border of the plate. Try to get an even distribution of the powder. Leave the plate to dry.

4 Make a second, denser, mixture of glue with bronze powder—this time purple. Use this to paint a thin edge around the rim of the plate and allow to dry.

5 Cut out the chocolates for your decoration. It is best to cut out more than you need, so that you can play around with the design until you achieve a pleasing result. Color the edges of your cutouts with a similar colored pencil or felt-tip pen (see page 17). Mark the final positions of the images with a sharp, hard pencil.

ARTIST'S TIP

If you can't find wrapping paper with chocolates, look at candy wrappers and boxes of chocolates.

6 Apply paste to the back of the prints one at a time and place them in their marked positions. Start with the most centrally positioned images, then radiate outward. Wipe off excess paste with a slightly damp sponge. Once completely dry, put on a face mask and spray-varnish the plate. Apply four coats, lightly sanding every second layer. Once the top is complete, don't forget to do the underside!

SEASHORE DRAWERS

It's not hard to transform a plain set of wooden drawers into a stylish piece of furniture. This project uses a combination of images taken from wrapping paper, napkins, and images from old books. The effect is to re-create a seaside scene.

YOU WILL NEED

- Small set of wooden drawers
- Fine sandpaper
- Face mask
- Muslin cloth
- Water-based primer
- Paintbrushes
- White and cream emulsion paints
- Shell wrapping paper
- Scissors
- Reusable putty
- Pencil
- Paste (see page 19)
- Spatula
- Sponge
- Seashore napkins
- Birds' egg color copies
- Flat decorators' varnish

1 Remove the drawers and give all surfaces a light sand before priming, wiping away any sanding dust with a muslin cloth first. Once the primer is dry, paint the drawers with white emulsion and the cabinet with cream. Allow to dry. Apply a second layer and lightly sand until smooth.

2 Cut out the shells from the wrapping paper and tack to the base drawer with reusable putty. Mark their positions with a sharp pencil. Then, one by one, paste them into position, smoothing out the paper with a spatula and removing excess paste with a slightly damp sponge. Add a seagull cut from a seashore napkin.

3 Tear out more images from the seashore napkins, and following the instructions on page 20, remove the backing tissue. Decide on an arrangement for the remaining drawers, then paste the appropriate areas and apply the tissue on top of the paste, one by one, smoothing them out carefully with a paintbrush.

4 Cut out the birds' egg color copies and paste into position to complement your arrangement.

5 Allow to dry, then coat the cabinet and drawers with flat decorators' varnish. This will give it a subtle finish. Apply four coats, lightly sanding between every second layer.

DESIGN VARIATION

This romantic set of drawers is painted in hot pink and purple. Flower wrapping paper surrounds it and Victorian scrap bunches of flowers decorate the drawers.

MAGAZINE RACK

The image on the front of this funky magazine rack has been cut out from leftover wallpaper. You can find similar images on the sides of store bags. Ask your wallpaper supplier to keep old sample books for you; they are a great resource for découpage.

YOU WILL NEED

- MDF blank or old magazine rack
- Fine sandpaper
- Face mask
- Decorators' filler
- Muslin cloth
- Water-based primer
- Paintbrushes
- Coral, hot pink, and yellow emulsion paints
- Two large flower prints
- Scissors
- Reusable putty
- Pencil
- Paste (see page 19)
- Spatula
- Sponge
- Cotton swabs
- Water-based varnish

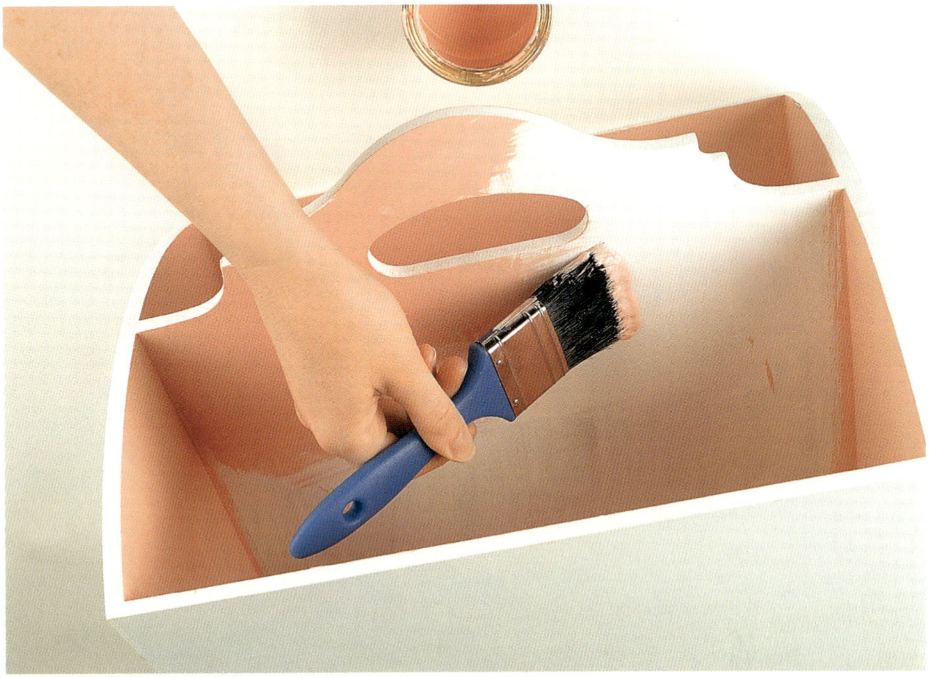

1 Check that your MDF blank is smooth and that the joints are tight. If it is rough in places, sand it before priming. If there are gaps in the joints, fill them with decorators' filler, sand and wipe with muslin, then prime. Once the top is dry, don't forget to prime the base. Paint the inside of the rack first—starting with the inside base—using the coral emulsion. It helps to have a long-handled brush for this job (such as a radiator brush). Leave the paint to dry, then lightly sand before applying a second coat.

2 Once the inside paintwork is dry, you can start on the outside using the hot pink emulsion. Stand the rack on a piece of wood to enable you to paint all around the bottom edge. Apply two coats.

3 When the hot pink emulsion has dried completely, paint the edges of the magazine rack yellow. Apply two coats. Once all the painting is dry, lightly sand the rack for a smooth finish.

4 Cut out your design carefully and tack it in position with reusable putty so that you can view it from a distance. When you are sure of its position, carefully mark around it with a pencil.

5 Spread paste on to the back of the print and position it on the rack. Smooth out any wrinkles with a spatula, radiating out from the center. Wipe over with a slightly damp sponge to remove excess paste. Use a cotton swab to remove any paste trapped between the "valleys" of the petals. Repeat this process on the opposite side of the rack.

6 Apply varnish to the finished rack, first to the inside and then to the outside. Once dry, give a light sand and repeat for the second coat. Apply six coats of varnish, lightly sanding between every second coat.

ARTIST'S TIP

Cover the rack with a big box when you are waiting for each layer of varnish to dry to keep dust from settling on it.

EASTER EGGS

It is an old Easter tradition to blow eggs and decorate them to hang on a branch. These lovely eggs have been pasted with images cut from Easter napkins (their thin tissue easily molds around an egg's curved surface) and have been painted with pastel acrylic paints and hung from bright silk ribbons.

YOU WILL NEED

- Blown white eggs (see Artist's Tip)
- Easter paper napkins
- Scissors
- Paste (see page 19)
- Paintbrushes
- Pastel acrylic paints
- Eggcup
- String
- Large box
- Spray varnish (matte or gloss)
- Face mask
- Long dollmaker's or upholstery needle
- Thin silk ribbon

ARTIST'S TIP

Using a needle, scratch a small cross at each end of the egg. Gradually etch the shell until you have created a small hole in the center of the cross. Jab around inside the egg with a long needle to break up the yolk, then blow from the broadest end of the egg. Once the egg is empty, wash it in soapy water, making sure the inside of the egg is thoroughly washed. Rub the surface of the egg with vinegar.

1 Choose your images from the napkins. Cut or tear them out and peel off the backing tissue (see page 20). Decide on the position of your images, then spread paste over the appropriate area on the egg, holding it carefully with your thumb and index finger at either end of the egg. Place the image on the glue and smooth out with a paintbrush (see page 20).

2 Once the glue is dry, you can paint the egg. Start by painting one end with a base color. Place the egg in an eggcup, the painted end on top, and leave it to dry. Repeat on the other end of the egg.

3 Using a fine brush, paint stripes of color around one end. Once dry, decorate these with patterns. Paint a flower around the end hole. Repeat at the opposite end.

4 When the body of the egg has been decorated, suspend it on a string in a large box and spray varnish in a well-ventilated room while wearing a face mask, or paint on varnish as described on page 22. When the varnish is dry, using the dollmaker's needle, thread up your silk ribbon and work it through from the bottom of the egg to the top. Make a loop at the top, and thread the needle back through the egg, tying the two ends of the ribbon in a knot at the bottom. Make sure that the knot is big enough not to slip into the egg.

DESIGN VARIATION

Blue and white is such a popular color combination to collect crockery in, so why not decorate some eggs to match? These motifs have all been cut from napkins.

POLKA DOT TRAY

Roses and polka dots are a very fashionable combination, and for this project I have found an easy alternative to painting dots. White self-adhesive dot stickers have been placed in position around the tray's sides. The roses are Victorian scraps (see pages 78–79 for details). Make sure to be generous with the layers of varnish for this project, as trays have to stand up to a lot of wear and tear.

YOU WILL NEED

- MDF blank tray
- Fine sandpaper
- Face mask
- Muslin cloth
- Water-based primer
- Paintbrushes
- Decorators' tape
- Blue, pink, and white emulsion paints
- White self-adhesive dot labels
- Pencil
- Small scissors
- Victorian rose scraps
- Paste (see page 19)
- Sponge
- Spatula
- Matte water-based varnish

1 Lightly sand the MDF blank and wipe the surface with a muslin cloth. Prime the top of the tray and allow it to dry. Once dry, turn it over and prime the sides and base.

2 Line the inside edge of the base of the tray with decorators' tape.

3 Paint the base of the tray blue with two coats of emulsion, sanding between layers. Once dry, remove the decorators' tape.

CHINTZ CHAIRS

These painted wooden chairs add a fresh feminine touch to any room. Choose floral fabrics to make the cushioned seats. A scan can be taken of the same fabric and used to make the découpage cutouts for the back of the chair. If you don't have access to a scanner, take the fabric to your nearest copy store to have a color copy made.

YOU WILL NEED

- Painted wooden chair
- Large sheet of scrap paper
- Pencil
- Scissors
- Old wool blanket
- Embroidery needle and thread
- Floral cushion fabric
- Sewing machine and thread
- Tape
- Needle and thread
- Color copy of fabric design
- Paintbrushes
- Paste (see page 19)
- Spatula
- Sponge
- Water-based varnish

1 If possible, remove the seat from the chair to make a pattern of it for the cushion. If you cannot do this, place a large piece of paper over the seat to trace its outline in pencil and cut it out.

2 Use the pattern to cut out three pieces from an old wool blanket to make the cushion filler.

3 Sandwich the three filler layers together and blanket stitch around all the raw edges with embroidery thread. Sew crosses here and there in the center of the "cushion filler" to stabilize the layers.

4 Fold the seat fabric in half, right sides together. Using the seat pattern and allowing an extra ½ in. all around, carefully cut out two pieces of fabric.

5 Tack and machine sew a ½ in. hem along the back edge of each piece of fabric. Tack the two pieces together, still right sides facing, incorporating two lengths of 15 in. tape at each of the front corners of the cushion cover. Machine sew the sides and front of the cover, leaving the back open for inserting the blanket filler. Trim any excess tape.

6 Turn the cushion cover right-side out and press. Cut two pieces of tape 25 in. long. Fold each in half and stitch at each corner of the back opening.

7 Place the blanket pad inside the cushion cover, then overstitch neatly along the back opening (this can be undone for washing the cover at a later time).

8 Make color copies or scans from a piece of the cushion fabric. Choose an area that will make a good motif for the back of the chair and cut it out.

9 Arrange the image on the chair, making sure that it fits neatly. Paste into position, smoothing over with a spatula, and wipe with a barely damp sponge. Allow to dry.

10 The backs of chairs get a lot of wear, so it is important that you apply a number of layers of varnish following the instructions on page 22. When the varnish is dry, you can use the tapes to secure the cushion to the chair. Adapt the size of the tape accordingly.

ARTIST'S TIP

You could also choose an image from your wallpaper to coordinate with your chairs.

JEWELRY BOX

Candy foil wrappers come in wonderful, tempting colors and can be used to create beautiful découpage. Care must be taken when varnishing foil, as some varnishes may remove the surface color.

YOU WILL NEED

- MDF jewelry box blank
- Masking tape
- Fine sandpaper
- Face mask
- Muslin cloth
- Water-based primer
- Paintbrushes
- Dark blue emulsion
- Pencil and ruler
- Confectionery foils
- Scissors
- White school glue
- Water-based varnish

1 Cover the hinges of the box with masking tape. Sand all surfaces and wipe over with a muslin cloth. Prime the box, leaving each section to dry completely before moving on to the next. Paint the inside of the box and lid with blue emulsion and leave to dry.

2 Now paint the outside edges of the lid, the base of the box, and its feet blue. Paint a second coat once the first is dry.

3 Measure all the dimensions of the box and cut a piece of foil to fit each side. Trim pieces to fit around any hinges. Glue into position.

CHRISTMAS BOX

Strong self-assembly storage boxes can be purchased. If you can't find one of these, use a stylish ready-made one. Victorian scraps and Christmas images from a copyright-free CD have been used to decorate this box. The original rope handles were replaced with a more suitable cord to complete the luxurious feel of the piece. Use the box to pack away your Christmas decorations or for transporting your presents.

YOU WILL NEED

- Self-assembly box (preferably)
- Water-based primer
- Paintbrushes
- Pencil and ruler
- Decorators' tape
- Green, red, and deep purple emulsion paints
- Cardboard
- Scissors
- Gold wrapping paper
- Paste (see page 19)
- Copyright-free images
- Victorian Christmas scraps
- Reusable putty
- Sponge
- Christmas border
- Thick gloss spray varnish
- Face mask
- Gold cord
- Three dimensional embossing paint

1 Prime the inside of the box and lid and allow to dry before priming the outsides. Using a pencil and ruler, mark out a 3 in. border around the top of the lid and a 2 in. border on each side of the box to give you a central panel on each visible surface. (The border widths can be adjusted according to the size of your box.) Mask off the borders with decorators' tape to paint the inside panel green. When dry, protect the green panel in the same way and paint the borders red.

2 Assemble the box and lid according to the manufacturer's instructions. Paint the inside of the box and lid with the purple emulsion. Allow to dry, then paint a second coat. Use the template on page 77 to draw and cut out a cardboard star. Use the template to cut stars from a sheet of gold wrapping paper. Paste them all over the interior of the box and lid at roughly regular intervals.

3 Choose the images you want to use from your copyright-free book or CD. Cut out the prints carefully and make a selection from your Victorian Christmas scraps. (An economic alternative is to use images cut out from Christmas wrapping paper.)

ARTIST'S TIP

You may prefer to use your favorite Christmas cards—this would be a great way to have them on display every Christmas.

4 Cut out the motifs for the panels on the sides of the box, allowing room for the holes that the cord handles will fit through. Taking each side one by one, tack the images to the green panel using reusable putty until you have the desired arrangement. Paste the images into position carefully, wiping each with a damp sponge to remove excess paste. Use little pictures where there are gaps and remember to leave room for the Christmas border.

5 Complete the design with a Christmas border, which finishes each panel with a clean edge. This one was enlarged 50 percent to fit the dimensions of the box. Position it and paste into place, wiping away excess paste with your sponge.

6 Choose the motifs for the lid of the box. Arrange within the green panel until you have achieved the desired result. Paste the images down and wipe clean any excess paste. Use the same or similar border, adjusted to the appropriate size, to complete the design.

7 Angels make a nice focus for the front panel of the box. Paste your chosen images according to your arrangement and surround them with a decorative border.

8 Once all the paste is dry, varnish the box—first the inside, then the outer surfaces. Use six to eight layers of thick, gloss spray varnish, sanding lightly between every second coat to achieve a smooth finish. Be sure to wear a face mask.

9 Thread your gold or silk cord through the holes in the side of the box, and cut the length accordingly—in this case it is 19 in. Tie a knot in both ends of the cord to ensure it does not slip out of the holes.

10 Use three-dimensional embossing paint to line the borders. It can be difficult doing long straight lines so make the lines slightly wiggly if you prefer.

TEMPLATES

Sky Screen (pages 56–59)

Set photocopier to 150 percent to copy images to correct size for project.

Christmas Box (pages 72–75)

Set photocopier to 150 percent to copy image to correct size.

SUPPLIERS

Aaron Brothers Art & Framing
1270 S. Goodrich Blvd.
Commerce, CA 90022
(888) 532-9371
www.aaronbrothers.com

Artcity.com
1350 Kelton Ave., Ste. 308
Los Angeles, CA 90024
(866) Artcity
www.artcity.com

The Art Store
455 Fortune Blvd.
Milford, MA 01757
(888) 5-GO-ARTS
www.artstores.com

Art Supply Warehouse
5325 Departure Dr.
Raleigh, NC 27616
(800) 995-6778
www.aswexpress.com

Decoupage Supply Centre
26650 County Road 46A
Sorrento, FL 32776
(352) 383-3883
www.3d-decoupage.com

Dove Brushes & Tools
1849 Oakmont Avenue
Tarpon Springs, FL 34689
(800) 334-DOVE
www.dovebrushes.com

G & S Dye and Accessories Ltd.
250 Dundas St. W. Unit #8
Toronto, ON, M5T 2Z5
Canada
www.gsdye.com

Jo-Ann Fabric & Crafts
5555 Darrow Rd.
Hudson, OH 44236
(800) 525-4951
www.joann.com

Michaels
8000 Bent Branch Dr.
Irving, TX 75063
(800) Michaels
www.michaels.com

MisterArt.com
1800 Peachtree St. NW, Ste. 250
Atlanta, GA 30309
(800) 423-7382
www.misterart.com

Photosphere Ltd.
Dept. 8110—Ste. 413
250 H Street
Blaine, WA 98230
(800) 665-1496
www.photosphere.com

PictureQuest
8280 Greensboro Drive, Ste. 520
McLean, VA 22102
(800) 764-7427
www.picturequest.com

Suzi's Wood Crafts Plus, Inc.
29895 N. Stampede Rd.
Athol, ID 83801
(888) 941-0044
www.suziswoodcrafts.com

Target
(888) 304-4000
www.target.com

Texas Art Supply
2001 Montrose Boulevard
Houston, TX 77006
(800) 888-9278
www.texasart.com

Vintage Postcards
312 Feather Tree Drive
Clearwater, FL 33765
(727) 467-0555
www.vintagepostcards.com

Acknowledgments
The author would like to thank:

Frederick Warne & Co.—controls all rights in the *Flower Fairies* books on behalf of the estate of Cicely Mary Barker.

The Medici Society for permission to use their fairies wrapping paper by Margaret Tarrant.

Pete Andrew and **Kathryn Hughes** at **WAVE**, Buckfastleigh, and **James Gillmore**, **John**, and **Eric** for their help with the computer.

Cath Lucroft Mee for use of the fabric bunting shown on pages 2 and 64.

Andrew Gillmore and **Heidi Green** for looking after Bryany during the photography.

The author would also like to thank the following companies for supplying materials for use in this book: **Appli Craft**, **Dover Publications Inc. (31 East 2nd St, Mineola, NY 11501, http://store. doverpublications.com/)**, **Mamelok Press Ltd**, **OPITEC Hobbyfix**, **Scumble Goosie**, **The Stencil House**, and **William Robinson**.

INDEX